INTRO

A few years after I graduated from college my life was a mess. Not a Living on the streets, drug-addled, can't hold down a job mess. Just a jumble of lazy choices and tracks headed nowhere. I had a job I didn't particularly like, a crappy apartment that cost way too much, I was getting fat and spending too much eating out all the time. I knew I needed a change but actually making one was somehow beyond me.

It's funny how inspiration can show up in the strangest places. I was reading a blog post about productivity one day while trying to kill time in my unsatisfying place of employment when I stumbled across the concept of "anti-goals". Basically making goals around the things that you want to avoid, instead of your desired outcomes. This simple (and probably intuitive for most people) concept resonated immediately.

Instead of saying "I want to lose weight", now I thought "How do I avoid getting fat and feeling awful?" By reversing the problem I had opened up a whole new set of solutions!

Within a year of reading about anti-goals, I had a new job and I was on my way to being in better financial and physical health. I've written several other books discussing how to apply the concept of anti-goals to various parts of your life.

It turns out that this amazing concept of anti-goals is just one of thousands of different Mental Models that can affect the way we see our world and allow us to make changes to it. I began to try to collect new mental models like tools in my mental toolbox. I was able to make amazing changes with just one tool, I imagined what

I could do with hundreds!

This book is by no means an all-encompassing guide to every mental model. It is based on the models I find the most useful in my daily life. Before we get too deep in the weeds I need to define...

What are Models?

A model is an abstraction and/or simplification of a system. Think of a dollhouse. It looks like a real house (only smaller) and has most of the same components. It might have kitchen appliances, even though they don't actually function. The dollhouse is a model of the real house and anyone familiar with a house will recognize it as such.

> *"Essentially, all models are wrong, but some are useful."* - George Box

Because a model is only an approximation it is inherently wrong, You can't turn on the stove in the dollhouse. But it can be useful or provide insight. Each model is a simplified version of some aspect of reality we want to learn more about. Imagine a map, it is a simplified abstract way to understand physical space. The map isn't exactly like the land it represents, but it can tell us valuable information area it represents.

So, what is so special about mental models? They are models designed to be conceived and simulated within a conscious mind. Instead of building a dollhouse, you are just imagining it, placing the rooms and furniture where they belong, picking out paint colors and other details. Mental models rely on existing knowledge to give them depth and meaning. If you don't understand what a refrigerator is you wouldn't know it belongs in the kitchen.

So far we have used mental models to describe a very basic physical object (a dollhouse), but they can do much more. The real beauty of understanding various models is that they allow you to simplify and understand more complex systems and concepts. Let's look at one of the most basic economic models as an example: supply and demand.

In ancient times people had no clue how the economy worked, as a result, there were constant food shortages. Inflation could run rampant any time a ruler felt like minting more coinage. Today we know more and live a more stable world as a result. This isn't the result of modern people being smarter, instead, over time cumulative knowledge accrued and models were formed based on events that took place. One of the most well-known and easiest to describe is supply and demand. If there is less bread available to be sold demand (and prices) go up. If there is too much bread available the demand goes down. While this model is a simplification it is instructive and can teach those using it something.

Building Your Toolbox

> "The first rule is that you've got to have multiple models—because if you just have one or two that you're using, the nature of human psychology is such that you'll torture reality so that it fits your models. And the models have to come from multiple disciplines because all the wisdom of the world is not to be found in one little academic department." - Charlie Munger

Every mental model you add is a tool in your toolbox. Some tools are great for one specific purpose, others can be used more generally. Imagine you are trying to build an entire house. You would need electrical tools and plumbing tools, tools for roofing and carpentry, as well as tools to work with drywall mud and cement for the basement. Having a broad set of mental models to draw from is equally important. If you only have economic models to draw upon you will look at everything in terms of cost and benefits. If you only have interpersonal tools you will focus on the human side of things, but ignore other issues. There is a mental model called Maslow's Hammer that fits well into this discussion, it states; "I suppose it is tempting, if the only tool you have is a hammer, to treat everything as if it were a nail."

Benefits of being a generalist

Having a broad range of knowledge is helpful in any field. The drawback of being too specialized is that you might not be able to see new or novel approaches to a problem. Applying models from one discipline to a completely unrelated field is usually where breakthroughs come from. To illustrate this think of the improvements in prosthetics for people missing a limb over the past decade. If the only way to address this issue was using standard medical models the gains would have been more limited. But, after drawing from robotics, neurological models and even biology amazing gains have been realized. Today fully articulated arms and hands are available. People missing a leg can run a marathon or go snowboarding. This is all due to science embracing a wider toolset and applying different models in unique ways.

Identifying Your Existing Models

The downside of mental models is that they can limit the way you see the world. Some can be downright harmful. Many people have developed an ingrained model to avoid or marginalize those who look different or speak a different language. While most people will agree that this is reprehensible, it is still a mental model. Identifying your existing models can be difficult, but it can also have as deep of an impact as adding new ones to your toolbox.

The author Dave Gray has come up with a concept called "liminal thinking", which is based on the idea that changing thoughts or belief can change behavior and, ultimately, your life. In its simplest form liminal thinking can be broken down into three principles:

    1. Understand your ignorance

2. Seek understanding
3. Do something different

If you aren't getting the results you want in an area of your life trying this simple exercise can make a profound difference. When most people say "I do it this way because I have always done it this way", you get the chance to reevaluate and make a change. Thinking about the "why" in your existing models and actions can have a similar result.

When this technique is coupled with adding other mental tools in this book the effects can be exponential.

How to use this book

I have organized this book into 8 chapters, each dealing with a different "discipline", and containing 3-5 models that I find relevant. I've written the word discipline in quotations because these are not organized by traditional fields of study, I've largely left the more math and science-based models out in favor of those with a broader range of use. Many of these models could have been included in multiple chapters.

For each model I will provide a definition, an example, and explain why it matters. As a bonus, I have also created a PDF listing each model, visit antigoals.net to download it. it is a brief description and a quote related to it to be used as a quick reference.

CHAPTER ONE: DECISION MAKING

I've elected to make the first chapter a group of mental tools focused on decision making and choice because these actions impact every aspect of life. Everything involves making decisions and choices. You are reading these words because you decided to buy this book, and you can make a choice to continue reading or put it down. How we react to different choices and the decision we make could be its own book of mental models.

Fast and Slow Thinking

"The idea that the future is unpredictable is undermined every day by the ease with which the past is explained." - Daniel Kahneman

This model is based on a concept (and book) by Nobel prize winner Daniel Kahneman. He argues that people make all of their decisions based on two different systems. System 1 is based on intuition and makes gut reactions based on first impressions, this is known as "fast thinking". System 2, or "slow thinking", is more of a critical thinking system, working through situations before making a choice.

While most people will tell you that they are generally system two thinkers the opposite is usually the case. According to Kahneman:

> "Systems 1 and 2 are both active whenever we are awake. System 1 runs automatically and System 2 is normally in comfortable low-effort mode, in which only a fraction of its capacity is engaged. System 1 continuously generates suggestions for System 2: impressions, intuitions, intentions, and feelings. If endorsed by System 2, impressions and intuitions turn into beliefs, and impulses turn into voluntary actions. When all goes smoothly, which is most of the time, System 2 adopts the suggestions of System 1 with little or no modification. You generally believe your impressions and act on your desires, and that is fine—usually.
>
> "When System 1 runs into difficulty, it calls on System 2 to support more detailed and specific processing that may solve the problem of the moment. System 2 is mobilized when a question arises for which System 1 does not offer an answer... System 2 is activated when an event is detected that violates the model of the world that System 1 maintains."

The problem with System 1 thinking is that because it is based on what is seen and that it tries to create a narrative, the results can be riddled with bias. "When information is scarce, which is a common occurrence, System 1 operates like a machine for jumping to conclusions."

Think of any conspiracy story you have ever heard. It probably was told as a story using only the facts supporting its conclusion. System 1 thinking often falls into this type of trap. Just by being aware of the problems posed by relying on system one thinking, one can realize when they are falling into the habit of fast thinking.

Kahneman offers an example in his book based on the price of a bat and ball. If the combined price of a bat and ball was $1.10 and you know that bat costs exactly $1.00 more than the ball, how much did the ball cost?....

If you used System 2 thinking and wrote the problem down and did the simple arithmetic you would have probably arrived at the correct answer: $0.05. However, most people reading this question use System 1 thinking and quickly say $0.10.

>System 1: Ball $0.10 + Bat $1.00 = $1.10, ~~Bat $1.00 - Ball $0.10 = $0.90~~
>System 2: Ball $0.05 + Bat $1.05 = $1.10, **Bat $1.05 - Ball $0.05 = $1.00**

Think of cable news, finance or sports programming. How often are the pundits, stock pickers, or sports experts right about the outcomes they are expounding? Our System 1 brain listens to them because they tell a story we can relate to. Based on a 2011 study (https://www.hamilton.edu/news/polls/pundit) done by Hamilton College, political pundits on major cable news were about as accurate at picking future outcomes as they would have been just flipping a coin.

Understanding the two decision-making systems is important

because it can help us to see bias for what it is, quick intuitive thought, that is often based on limited or incorrect information.

Loss Aversion and Risk Aversion

"Every nut the squirrel hoards is another it's afraid to lose." - Marty Rubin

Loss Aversion refers to the psychological principle that people tend to prefer avoiding loss instead of acquiring similar gains. This means that most people would work harder to avoid losing $5 than they would to make the same amount. Think of anything you have ever purchased after being given a free trial. You get hooked on the product or service and you would rather part with money than be without it going forward.

Loss aversion also hinges on the sunk cost fallacy. People will continue to send good money after bad, even though they know it is a losing cause. In poker, inexperienced players will continue to call even though they have an extremely low probability of winning, due to the fact that they already have committed money to the pot.

Risk aversion is different from loss aversion. Risk implies that you are operating with incomplete information and tries to decide how likely a negative outcome is to occur. Being more loss averse can actually lead you to be less risk-averse. Imagine you have $100 and are completely loss adverse. Instead of investing you would keep it as cash in a safe for the next ten years. In that time inflation goes up so after ten years your $100 can actually buy less than it would be able to if it had been invested in a savings account at the bank. Due to a fear of losing money you have actually lost money.

The opposite is also true. The billionaire investor, Warren Buffett, once offered to underwrite a one billion dollar prize being offered by Pepsi as part of an advertising campaign. The contest was set up in such a way that the odds of anyone winning were 1 in 1 billion. Still, in order to lay off the risk, Pepsi decided to take out an insurance policy against anyone potentially winning the prize. Warren Buffett's company, Berkshire Hathaway, agreed to assume the risk for $10 million. The agreement was structured so that Pepsi paid Berkshire Hathaway $10 million, and that if anyone won the contest Berkshire Hathaway would be responsible for paying out the entire Billion dollars. This is an example of being risk averse but not loss averse because Warren Buffett understood the basic math and law of probability underlying the issue. The risk (one in one billion) of losing $1 billion had such a low probability of happening, that taking $10 million made sense.

When making decisions where you can potentially lose always figure out if you are avoiding (or minimizing) risk. Know where the gaps in your knowledge lie and how likely they are to affect you. Are you avoiding risk or loss based on the decision you make?

Confirmation Bias

> *"People put a lot less effort into picking apart evidence that confirms what they already believe."* - Peter Watts

Confirmation bias is the human tendency to look for facts and evidence to support our existing positions. Imagine I was to tell you that I believe the world is flat. I might point to the fact that a pencil on my desk doesn't roll off, or that the surface of a pond looks completely smooth as evidence of my theory. Obviously, most of us know that the world isn't flat and that I am just cherry picking observations to support my claim. Confirmation bias can work in more subtle ways as well.

As we discussed earlier in the chapter System 1 thinking can be a form of confirmation bias. If you don't exercise slow thinking your brain will quickly form a story of what is happening, and decisions will be made to fit with that narrative.

Another trap that confirmation bias can set is the self-fulfilling prophecy. This happens when a person's beliefs affect their behavior is subtle ways that actually lead to the imagined outcome. This can work in both positive and negative ways. "Fake it until you make it" is an often repeated quote for those trying to climb the ladder in the entertainment industry, referring to projecting an air of success that (hopefully) becomes actual success one day. On the other side, someone convinced that a calamity is going to happen to them might take subconscious steps ensuring that it actually does.

In his book, "Research in Psychology: Methods and Design," C. James Goodwin gives an example of confirmation bias related to believers in extrasensory perception (ESP).

> "Persons believing in extrasensory perception (ESP) will keep close track of instances when they were 'thinking about Mom, and then the phone rang and it was her!' Yet

they ignore the far more numerous times when (a) they were thinking about Mom and she didn't call and (b) they weren't thinking about Mom and she did call. They also fail to recognize that if they talk to Mom about every two weeks, their frequency of "thinking about Mom" will increase near the end of the two-week-interval, thereby increasing the frequency of a 'hit.'"

When making decisions it's important to be aware of confirmation bias. We are all operating based on previous experiences and that information is necessary to get anything done, but it can be used in such a way to exclude possible choices if we aren't careful. Keep in mind that confirmation bias works in the rearview as well, in the form of memory bias. Events are remembered in such a way as to support preconceived notions. Often admitting that there may be some level of bias is enough to mitigate it.

Paradox of Choice

"The hardest decisions in life are not between good and bad or right and wrong, but between two goods or two rights." – Joe Andrew

Everyone wants to have more choices, right? Psychologist Barry Schwartz argues the opposite in his book, "The Paradox of Choice – Why More Is Less". His main point is that in the modern world we have too many options to choose from and that the volume of choices we have to make today limit our time and mental capacity to do other things. To illustrate this point I went to the drug store to buy toothpaste today. There were 26 different options to choose from! If I were to weigh all the different choices based on packaging, price, size, benefits, etc. I would be standing in the toothpaste aisle for an hour!

According to Schwartz' research consumers follow a 6 step process when making a decision.
1. Figuring out the goal - I want toothpaste so my teeth are white and don't fall out of my head, I also don't want to spend too much
2. Evaluating the importance of the goal - Not very, if I were buying a new car I would put much more thought into the process
3. Array the options - There are a bunch of different types of toothpaste, but I also have an option of buying nothing and having bad teeth.
4. Evaluate how well each option can meet your goals - This involved looking at the packaging and price tags for a few minutes
5. Pick a winning option - I went with 10 oz of Crest Whitening Mint
6. Modify goals - This step takes place after the choice is made and helps inform future choices. If I hate the flavor of this toothpaste next time I will be less likely to

buy Crest.

The example I just provided was for a shopping trip I made for one product that was very unimportant to me. Imagine the mental bandwidth that can go into shopping for a family of four every week at the grocery store!

The paradox of choice can be seen everywhere we look. 20 years ago cable television had 30 channels. Today my Directv subscription gives me access to over 300 channels, and I still can't find anything to watch.

To see the opposite of too many choices being used effectively look at Trader Joe's supermarkets. Today they are one of the fastest growing and most popular chains of supermarkets, mainly for the reason that they don't offer too much choice. If you have ever been in a Trader Joe's you know they have one type of canned corn and only one option for triangle corn chips. If you walk in with a shopping list and a plan you have to expend very little mental energy choosing between different brands (because there aren't any).

In a related way not making choices can also be attributed to having too many options. "I don't want to make plans because something better may come up", is one way to look at it. This also relates to the recently popular term FOMO (fear of missing out).

As you can see having too many choices can be worse than having limited options. As technology improves this is unlikely to go away any time soon. The easiest way to combat too much choice is to improve your goal setting and importance evaluation (the first two steps in the list above). If we go back to my toothpaste example I already know I don't like any cinnamon flavored toothpaste, so I am able to automatically eliminate those from my selection process.

CHAPTER TWO: DEALING WITH OTHERS

We all have to deal with other people to get anything done in life. Originally I was going to call this chapter "understanding others" but that didn't quite fit. Some of the models are designed to understand what someone else is doing or thinking. Others are built around relating to or even influencing them. Chapter 6 in this book deals with negotiation, but these models are also helpful in influencing others to get your desired outcome.

Hanlon's Razor

"Never attribute to malice that which is adequately explained by stupidity."

This is my favorite quote and model for relating to anyone I feel has wronged me. I was driving the other day and as I was about to merge onto the highway a car cut me off. I was livid! I honked and tailgated them. When I had a chance to pass I pulled up alongside and I felt like an idiot. It was an extremely old woman who looked terrified!

I assumed that the other driver was out to get me, and was being a jerk cutting me off. In reality, the old woman probably shouldn't have been driving, but her lack of intent to harm me changed my attitude completely.

While this is one of the shortest and most easily explained models in this book it is also one of the most powerful. Another way to look at it is to not take things personally. Getting emotional about a situation can end up limiting options and invoking more System 1 thinking. Always try to stay above an instant emotional response, especially before you know the other person's true intentions.

Ad Hominem

"I always cheer up immensely if an attack is particularly wounding because I think, well, if they attack one personally, it means they have not a single political argument left." - Margaret Thatcher

Ad hominem is a Latin phrase meaning "to the man" and is the practice of insulting an opponent personally instead of arguing their position. In modern politics, this has recently become the norm, with little time being spent on issues and most of the time trying to undermine an opponent's credibility.

The problem with ad hominem is that it provides little to no value in terms of reaching a resolution. If I support position A and you support position B, and instead of debating the merits of each we call each other idiots no change or resolution is possible.

Ad hominem has several other variations.

Tu quoque translates to "you also" and it is used when the source of the argument has already acted in a contradictory manner to their own position. As an example, if I tell you that smoking causes cancer and then you point out that I used to smoke, it doesn't make my statement any less true.

Circumstantial ad hominem is when you refute an argument because of the source's personal circumstances. If I tell you that my neighbor is a great barber, you refute the point because I am bald, and therefore, do not understand what makes a great barber.

Guilt by association is also a form of ad hominem. Group A makes claim B. Group C also makes claim B. Due to similar claims both groups are seen as related. In politics, we see variations of this all the time, "My opponent just received the endorsement of (insert politically damaging endorsement here), is this really the person you want representing you?"

While it can be satisfying to personally attack an opponent, and in some cases advantageous, make sure you know the difference between a personal attack and one based on issues. If you have to continue working with someone, especially outside the arena of politics, using ad hominem can be a dangerous game. On the other hand, if someone is attacking you personally in a debate, it can be due to the fact that they don't have a strong position.

Entropy

"you can't unscramble an egg"

I'm borrowing the model of entropy from thermodynamics, specifically the *Third Law of Thermodynamics*, which states:

> "that the total entropy of an isolated system can never decrease over time. The total entropy can remain constant in ideal cases where the system is in a steady state (equilibrium), or is undergoing a reversible process. In all spontaneous processes, the total entropy always increases and the process is irreversible. The increase in entropy accounts for the irreversibility of natural processes, and the asymmetry between future and past."

So, what does this have to do with interpersonal interactions? Actually quite a bit it turns out. Entropy says that over time certain irreversible processes happen that cannot be undone. It also says without expending energy things tend to become more disordered.

Dealing with others can be seen through the lens of entropy in several ways.

There are ways that you can treat others that can cause permanent damage and are irreversible. If you do something terrible to someone, don't expect them to help you in the future. Keeping this idea in mind can help you avoid potential mistakes. As we all know the arrow of time only points in one direction, so actions you take now have future consequences.

Maintaining relationships takes energy. Over time if you don't keep in touch friendships break down and erode. I haven't spoken to my college roommate in over two years, even though we used to live together and were best friends. Without expending energy the entropy increased.

When relationships break down they can take more energy to fix if repair is even possible. Understanding that as time progresses entropy in any system will continue to increase is a helpful perspective to understand your dealing with others.

Theory of Influence

"There are two parts to influence: First, influence is powerful; and second, influence is subtle. You wouldn't let someone push you off course, but you might let someone nudge you off course and not even realize it." - Jim Rohn

This model is actually six key principles of influence, based on the work of psychology and marketing professor Robert Cialdini. He has also written several best selling books on the concept of influence and persuasion. The following six principles show the factors that get others to say "yes". Understanding each, and using it in an ethical way can greatly improve your chances of getting to a favorable outcome in any social situation or negotiation.

1. **Reciprocity** - Or to quote an old phrase "you get what you give". This is the concept that people will generally give back to someone who has given them something. If I invite you to my party, the next time you throw a party of your own there is a good chance I'll be on the guest list. To leverage this principle effectively be the first to give something in an interaction, and make sure it is something unexpected.
2. **Scarcity** - People always want what is hard to get. This is the reason limited time offers, and holiday sales work. If you know a product will become unavailable shortly, or that the price is going to go up, you will try to buy it now. In interpersonal relationships limiting your exposure can have a similar effect, "I haven't seen Joe in a while, he's probably doing something interesting..."
3. **Authority** - When someone in a position of authority makes a request the majority of people will comply. This works fine if you are a cop and your uniform is able to convey your authority, or a doctor and the diploma on the wall of your office speaks to your authority, but

what about for the rest of us? Some options are listing credentials on business cards or websites, or having others introduce you with a short description of your accomplishments.
4. **Consistency** - If you get someone to agree with you on one item, it is easier to get them to agree to something else. This is why used car dealers ask questions that are always answered in the affirmative, it establishes the pattern of saying "yes". This principle works because people like to be consistent with the things they have previously done.
5. **Liking** - If you like the messenger you are more apt to like the idea. This principle explains why attractive salespeople generally do better than their less attractive counterparts. It is also responsible for the prevalence of small talk in the sales profession. Establishing a personal relationship, no matter how superficial, increases the likelihood of a successful outcome.
6. **Social Proof** - When people are uncertain they will look to the actions of others to inform their decisions. This is why phrases like "People in your area are..." or "90% of your neighbors currently are... " are being deployed to get people to be responsible citizens. These tactics are being used to increase voter turnout and recycling programs. In interpersonal situations, this can be used as well.

These six simple principles can be modeled in many different ways to allow you to increase your success in dealing with other people.

CHAPTER THREE: EXPLAINING AND UNDERSTANDING

To explain something fully you have to understand it. I also find the opposite to be true; to be able to understand something I find it helps to try to explain it to someone else, or even just myself. In the explanation, I usually find the holes in my theory or limits to my knowledge. This chapter has five models that have helped me to sharpen my ability to understand and explain.

Occam's Razor

"The explanation requiring the fewest assumptions is most likely to be correct." - William of Ockham

This is probably the most well-known model in this book. Occam's Razor states that the simplest solution is probably the correct one. While it isn't a universal truth or proven scientific method, it can provide value as a model in the real world.

If I am prone to losing my keys (which I am), and my keys aren't where I thought I left them, which is more probable?: A) that I misplaced my keys again, or B) that someone broke into my house and stole my keys, but nothing else?

According to Occam's Razor option A is more likely, and thus probably the correct solution. It actually was correct, I left the keys in my car...

This model was first developed by William of Occam in the 14th century. He was a Franciscan monk and philosopher with an interest in logic. The term Razor was added since his theory involved shaving away complicated solutions, or extra steps in a solution to reach the simplest possible explanation.

In addition to solving problems, this mental model can also be used in day to day choices. Have you ever wondered why Barack Obama only wore a blue or grey suit when he was president? Or why Mark Zuckerberg only wears grey t-shirts and hoodies? Its because they each face so many decisions in a day that not having to choose an outfit makes each day a little easier. This strategy of simplifying and limiting choice can be used by anyone. Try eating the same lunch every day if you want to lose weight, or set your bills to auto-pay every month to simplify your personal finances. Simplification allows you to avoid decision fatigue and can generate side benefits if done correctly.

Murphy's Law and Hofstadter's Law

This section is a two for one because I find these models to be complementary. Before going into each of these models I can sum them up in a short story.

Last year I purchased a house. It was old and run down, but I got it cheap and I had big plans to fix it up myself. I have friends who are contractors so I got some advice from them and started drawing up plans on what I would change, how much materials would cost, what I would need to hire help for, and how long it would take. I even built in some added budget and time for unforeseen complications. I bet you can guess what happened... Two months after I was planning on being finished and moved in it was still far from complete. I was also $10,000 over budget. So what happened?

<u>Murphy's Law</u>: "Anything that can go wrong will go wrong".

<u>Hofstadter's Law</u>: "It always takes longer than you expect, even when you take into account Hofstadter's Law."

It is easy to relate both of these models back to entropy, or the prevalence of any system to trend to disorder over time. While I was working on the house I discovered that all of the plumbing leaked. Over time the pipes had gone bad due to lack of maintenance. Nobody was putting in the energy to prevent the slide toward disorder.

You could make the argument that not "everything" that could possibly go wrong with the house did, in fact, go wrong. The roof was in generally fine condition and didn't need any work, the electrical systems and wiring were good, and all of the appliances were in working order. However, on a long enough timeline, with no upkeep, all of the items would have required replacement or repair.

Just being aware that problems will occur and planning for them is the basis of these models. While it is impossible to accurately predict the future, it is a near certainty that problematic situations will arise. Having a plan in place for dealing with issues and the flexibility to address them can often be the difference between success and failure.

Counterfactual Thinking

"So we have the paradox of a man shamed to death because he is only the second pugilist or the second oarsman in the world. That he is able to beat the whole population of the globe minus one is nothing; he has "pitted" himself to beat that one; and as long as he doesn't do that nothing else counts." - William James

Counterfactual thinking is something that everyone does. Every time you say to yourself "if only I had done..." or "what if..." you are engaging in thinking that is counter to the facts. Because the arrow of time only points in one direction it is impossible to realize these different choices. In some ways, it can be counterproductive.

Just think about the character of Uncle Rico in the movie Napoleon Dynamite. He was focused on how much better his life would have been had he played quarterback in high school (despite all evidence pointing to him being terrible at it). *"How much you wanna make a bet I can throw a football over them mountains?... Yeah... Coach woulda put me in fourth quarter, we would've been state champions. No doubt. No doubt in my mind."*

Counterfactual thinking has two portions, activation and content. Activation is when counterfactual thought seeps into conscious thought, content is the imagined possible outcome. Counterfactual thinking is prevalent in two types of situations, when exceptional circumstances lead to an event, or when we feel guilty about a specific outcome. As an example imagine my house burned down, three days after I forgot to renew my insurance policy! This is both an exceptional circumstance, and something I would feel very guilty about. The counterfactual thought could be something like "If I had renewed my policy I would be rich", or "If this had happened last week I would be fine".

Counterfactual thinking can also explain why Olympic Bronze medalists are generally happier than those who win Silver. According to a 1995 study in the Journal of Personality and Social Psychology, titled "When Less is More", it has been shown that Silver medalists are generally upset at not having won Gold. Their counterfactual thoughts tend to be focused on what if they had won. On the other hand, Bronze medalists are generally euphoric at just being on the podium. They focus their counterfactual thoughts down, towards what would have happened if they came in 4th or even lower.

Counterfactual thinking can also be seen having strange effects in the workplace. Imagine I give you a 5% raise this year, it would feel pretty good, right? Now imagine you find out I also gave your co-worker a 20% raise (and he doesn't even work as hard as you do). What was initially a happy outcome now has you confused and full of counterfactual thought.

As humans, it is impossible to completely turn off counterfactual thinking. In order to use this model to your advantage, it is important to understand why humans have evolved counterfactual thinking. Learning from a situation that has already occurred is easier (and safer) to game out different possible outcomes than to wait and act each out when a new chance presents itself. If you are a prehistoric hunter/gather and your buddy Dave gets sick from eating the red berries, it is better to imagine yourself getting sick from eating those berries than to test them yourself.

Using our imagination in a counterfactual way allows us to reach new levels of creativity, or helps us gauge probability better. The negative consequences of counterfactual thought occur when emotions like guilt, blame, and regret are brought into the mix.

Knowing the difference between learning and fixating on emotional events that cannot be changed are key to using this mental model.

Parkinson's Laws

If you have ever had a school assignment with a deadline in the distant future you already understand Parkinson's first law.

> *"Work expands so as to fill the time available for its completion."* - Cyril Northcote Parkinson

Cyril Northcote Parkinson was a British bureaucrat in the mid-1900's. His "Laws" are derived from an article he wrote in The Economist in 1955, explaining how the British bureaucracy grew every year, regardless of the amount of work that needed to be (or was actually) done. In addition to the first law mentioned above, he also posited two others: *"Expenditure rises to meet income"*, and *"Expansion means complexity, and complexity decay."*

While Parkinson was using these laws to describe giant government functions, they are equally applicable to everyday life. Let's discuss each in turn and how they can be used as beneficial mental models.

The first law shows that regardless of how long you have to complete a task, the task will take all of the available time. In some ways, this is contradictory to Hofstadter's Law, which we discussed earlier in the chapter. Assuming the task CAN be completed in the allotted time, then any additional time assigned to it is superfluous.

To take advantage of this law you need to figure out how much time is actually needed for a task, and then assign only that amount. Setting hard deadlines (often before something is actually due to be completed) compresses work time and can yield better results. I can remember college papers I wrote the night before they were due (after ignoring them for weeks) as being some of my best work.

The second law, dealing with spending rising to meet earnings, can be seen anytime a person gets a raise at work. I currently earn much more than I did in my early 20's, but my spending has also gone up to match. One way to combat this is to understand what is happening. If you have a goal to save money, make a rule to put away a certain percentage of any increase in earnings automatically. Since the percentage of the increased pay is never realized in your bank account it will not be missed.

The third law, "Expansion means complexity, and complexity decay," can be seen as a function of entropy, which we have discussed already. The larger something is the more complex it becomes. The more complex something is the more effort is required to maintain it.

This law can be looked at in two ways. First, if you keep adding complexity to your life or business it will eventually begin to collapse. Or, secondly, if you do continue to add complexity expect to have to invest an equally large amount into maintenance to avoid decay.

Let's look at an example to demonstrate the 2nd and 3rd laws. Imagine you win the lottery tomorrow and you have always wanted to have a giant yacht. You were never able to afford a yacht before, but now it is within your means. You buy the yacht, but it is too big for you to drive, so you have to hire a captain. The engines require constant work so a mechanic is also needed. You're too rich to wash it yourself, so a crew is hired. Now in addition to the cost of the yacht, you also have a staff you need to pay in order to use it and keep it in good condition. Your expenses have expanded, and so has the level of complexity. If you suddenly lost all of your money and were unable to sell the yacht, it would quickly fall into disrepair.

Most people never understand that they will take all the time given to complete a task, spend up to (and often beyond) their income, and increase complexity until it comes to the point of collapse. By understanding these simple models it makes it easier to explain poor allocations of time and financial resources.

CHAPTER FOUR: CREATIVITY

No matter what you do having the ability to be creative is a benefit. The problem has always been, "what can I do to be more creative?" This chapter is made up of 3 mental models that help you think outside the box and view problems in new and novel ways. It isn't a complete guide to the creative process, instead, it offers tricks and methods to get your creative juices flowing.

Lateral Thinking

"Do not seek to follow in the footsteps of the men of old; seek what they sought." - Matsuo Basho

"Lateral Thinking" was created by Edward De Bono in his book of the same name. It is a method broken up into 7 techniques, that aims to generate creative and useful ideas and solutions for a problem. Instead of using the classical linear idea of problem-solving, lateral thinking looks for new perspectives and different ways to approach the problem.

Picture McGyver from the 90's TV series. He would find himself in difficult situations with a roll of duct tape, a car antenna, some antacid tablets and by looking at these items from a different perspective come up with an invention to get himself out of a jam. Instead of playing the game with the pieces he had, he made up entirely new pieces and a new game.

The 7 techniques of Lateral thinking are:

1. **Alternatives** - By generating new concepts or aspects of concepts to focus on you can come up with new ideas.
2. **Focus** - Changing your focus onto a different part of a problem can yield results that would not have been considered otherwise.
3. **Challenge** - By challenging established ways of doing things new solutions (and more questions) can present themselves.
4. **Random Entry** - Uses random words, ideas, or groups to make you think outside the box and can lead to new and different connections.
5. **Provocation** - By provoking new and original ideas and applying them to a problem it is possible to build a larger list of possible solutions to consider. This can be done by taking a break or doing something else and allowing the mind to wander.

6. **Harvesting** - Done toward the end of the process, this is where ideas are reshaped into practical solutions.
7. **Treatment of Ideas** - Shaping ideas to fit the constraints of the problem and reality. A good idea cannot be realized if it is impossible.

De Bono also argued that lateral thinking is responsible for humor. What makes something funny is that it unexpected, and also switches the listeners thinking from a familiar pattern to a new and unexpected one. Here are a couple examples:

Q: There is a basket with 6 eggs in it. Six people each take one egg. How can there still be one egg left in the basket?

A: The last person took the basket with the egg in it.

Q: Responding to a tip that a murder has been seen entering a house the police arrive. They do not know what the murder looks like, but they do know his name is John. Upon entering the house they find a carpenter, a firefighter, a bus driver, and a car mechanic all playing cards. Without saying anything they immediately arrest the firefighter. How do they know they have the right suspect?

A: All the others are women

Q: Once there was a recluse who lived by himself. He never had visitors and never allowed anyone inside his home. One night, during a terrible storm, he had a nervous breakdown. He went upstairs and turned off all of the lights and went to bed. In the morning he had caused the deaths of hundreds of people. How is this possible?

A: He lived in a lighthouse

Breakthroughs occur when assumptions are broken. We can see this repeated throughout history. They also seem obvious when looking back at them. Take the example of Steve Jobs at Apple.

Now, when we look back at all of the success it seems obvious that everyone wants to have a little computer phone in their pocket, but at the time many people thought it wouldn't take off. Steve Jobs' genius was to see that people didn't want more buttons and jargon. They didn't want to know the specs of their computers. They just wanted something simple and user-friendly, not something that made them feel stupid or like an outsider when they used it.

Another way to think about lateral thinking can be seen by looking at the old saying "the shortest path between two points is a straight line". If there are too many people standing in that line, wouldn't it be faster to simply walk around them?

Inversion

"A lot of success in life and business comes from knowing what you want to avoid: Early death, a bad marriage, etc..." - Charlie Munger

Inversion is the process of taking a problem and flipping it upside down in order to see it from a new perspective. Instead of asking "what is the best way to do X?", you could invert the question by saying, "what is the worst thing I could do for X, and how do I avoid that?" My first book, Anti-Goals, was dedicated to this concept.

The premise is that it is easier to think about what you want to avoid, rather than what you want to achieve. Imagine you want to lose weight. A traditional goal might be, "I want to lose ten pounds". While this is somewhat specific, it doesn't give a roadmap for achievement. Instead, think about the problem in reverse, what are the things you are trying to avoid? Perhaps you don't want to get tired when playing with your kids, or you are trying to avoid diabetes. By reframing the problem you can come up with more defined steps to reach your desired outcome.

By saying "I want to lose ten pounds" you have infinite options to get that result. You could do it through many different types of exercise programs, hundreds of different diets, or a combination of diet and exercise. As we covered earlier in the Paradox of Choice, if options are unlimited they are more difficult to choose and this makes you more likely to fail.

By reframing the question, and looking at it through inversion clearer options appear. If you don't want to get tired when playing with your kids you probably need more exercise. Finding a program that will get you in shape for the level of activity you anticipate is far simpler than the all-encompassing goal of "lose some weight". If you are trying to avoid diabetes a conversation with your doctor can probably provide all the information you need to get started on a healthier path.

I've placed this mental model in the creativity section of the book because I find that this exercise can also be helpful for breaking through mental roadblocks and finding novel solutions. I actually used it when having the cover designed for this book. In addition to finding examples of other book covers I liked, I also made a list of book covers I hated. Based on the ones I didn't like I knew I didn't want a photo on the cover. I knew which fonts didn't match my concept, and I knew I wanted to keep it fairly clean and uncluttered.

Next time you have any trouble coming up with creative ideas, try doing the opposite. Come up with the worst possible solution, and then think of ways to avoid it.

Addition Through Subtraction

"The soul grows by subtraction, not addition." - Henry David Thoreau

In the world today you can find out anything about anything. There is plenty of information out there, completely free for the taking. If your goal is to make something that people want, try using subtraction instead of adding more to the pile of human knowledge. Think about the book you are reading right now. To create it I had to read thousands of pages, internalize all of these mental models, and then condense them each into a sub-chapter in an interesting (at least I hope) way. My creative process involved subtracting extraneous information and adding my own spin to the material.

Most people think that creativity involves creating something entirely new, or applying paint to a fresh canvas. In reality, most ideas have already seen the light of day. Being creative is also involved in repackaging or reimagining a great idea, simplifying it or applying it to a different purpose.

In his book, "Steal Like an Artist", Austin Kleon writes:

> "Creativity is subtraction. Not 'addition'. Choose what to leave out. There is massive information overload. It's too easy to add stuff, instead of simplifying, cleaning and reducing complexity. Think first about all the stuff you can leave out. How many words did Dr. Seuss use, in Cat in the Hat? 236! Why? Because his editor asked for such a book. And he discovered subtraction was his secret weapon."

Earlier we discussed entropy, and that the more complex something becomes the more difficult it is to maintain. By subtracting and simplifying you can create something that is faster, less expensive, more reliable, and more profitable.

Instead of thinking about what features you can add to a product,

Mental Models

what new chapters or passages you can add to a book, or what new services you can offer at your business, take a look at what you can remove. MIndlessly cutting can have a negative effect, but when done in the correct mindset, subtraction can be one of the most powerful creative tools available.

Think about any Apple product. They have been engineered to be simple and intuitive to use. Compared to earlier computers they give the user much less access to technical systems and less ability for the tech-savvy among us to change the core operating system, but they are simple to use. My new MacBook didn't even come with instructions. When I turned it on the computer gave me a short tutorial and I was off and running with it. By subtracting features that the majority of users didn't want (or even understand) Apple was able to make devices for the masses that are easy to understand and operate.

CHAPTER FIVE: REASONING

I debated adding a chapter on reasoning to this book because any mental model can be said to involve a form of reasoning. I decided to go forward with this chapter since several of my favorite models fall into this category but offer broader implications than just decision making. Reasoning is the act of thinking about something in an ordered and logical way. These are some of the models with the broadest range of applications in the book.

Anecdotal Reasoning

"Polls Are Inaccurate In My Opinion, Based Upon Anecdotal Evidence, Based Upon People That I Know." — Herman Cain (Former Presidential Candidate)

An anecdote is a short story told in the first person about an event. Anecdotal evidence is the story someone tells that provides information or a conclusion. The problem with anecdotal evidence is that it takes a single point of view into account, and is not held to the same rigorous standards that scientific evidence is.

Imagine I ask a friend what diet she is doing because she has lost weight. Even if she tells me everything she has done and I follow her advice to the letter there is no reason to think I will respond the same way to her protocol. Everyone's body is different and can respond in different ways. There is no reason to logically conclude that her diet will give me the same results.

The problem with anecdotal evidence is that we are hardwired to listen to it. Thousands of year ago, when humans lived in small groups, it wasn't possible to run a statistically sound survey or conduct a controlled experiment to get accurate data. Anecdotal evidence was what was available, and it's what we used.

There are plenty of situations where anecdotal evidence can be helpful. If I ask a friend for a referral for what plumber they used, or if they liked a new restaurant, I am likely to have a similar positive experience.

Anecdotal evidence becomes malicious when it is cherry picked to support a conclusion. In 2017 there was a health fad centered on the belief that coconut oil was good for almost anything and anyone. "Want to lose weight, or improve your skin? Try Coconut Oil!" This trend had increasing coconut oil consumption as the answer. Hundreds of bloggers wrote about their diets filled with coconut oil. There was ever a movement that encouraged people to add coconut oil and butter to their coffee, claiming it caused weight loss.

The problem was that almost all of the supporting evidence was anecdotal. According to the article published by NBC News, "Health Hero or Dietary Disaster":

> The truth is, there just isn't a lot of hard evidence to warrant the health halo that coconut oil has been crowned with. The general guidelines from health organizations haven't changed in regards to saturated fat, and much of the support behind the "superfood" status of coconut oil is anecdotal, lacking concrete scientific evidence. So it's best to err on the side of caution when incorporating it into your diet.

While coconut oil might have health benefits, the scientific jury is still out. Instead of taking unproven dietary advice from dubious sources it's often better to follow a more logical approach to getting information.

Understanding how anecdotal evidence works can give you a big advantage when giving and receiving information. By accepting that any information given to you in the form of a personal story or recommendation should be treated with a healthy dose of skepticism, you can avoid blindly following trends that may not have any benefit to you. On the flip-side, you know that people are generally preprogrammed to add enormous weight to any personal recommendation they receive. Just think about the reviews you read in Amazon. How do you know that the person leaving the review is an expert, or even has similar taste to yours? Yet you are predisposed to give weight to what they have to say about a product.

Correlation vs. Causation

"One of the first things taught in introductory statistics textbooks is that correlation is not causation. It is also one of the first things forgotten." — Thomas Sowell

Before discussing why correlation does not equal causation it is important to define both terms.

Correlation is a mutual relationship between two or more things. For example, people who are taller generally weigh more. Height and weight are correlated. This isn't always true though. Sometimes a tall person is extremely thin, or a short person is overweight.

Causation is a relationship of dependence between two or more things. For B to happen A has to happen first. The gun fired (B) because the trigger was pulled (A).

The obvious problem is that people automatically see two things that seem to be related and automatically try to figure out how one factor is causing the other (correlation = causation). To see this in action consider this; when ice cream consumption goes up, so do incidents of skin cancer diagnosis. Does ice cream cause skin cancer?

Of course not, they are correlated because they both happen in the summer. It is hot so people eat more ice cream. People are also outside in the sun more often, leading to increases in skin cancer.

By assuming that all correlated things have a causal effect it is possible to make statistics come up with many types of misinformation. There is a funny example that correlates the number of swimming pools drownings every year to the number of Nicolas Cage films released. Nobody believes the star of Con Air is actually causing drownings, but it can be statistically linked.

To avoid falling into the correlation/causation trap it is important to do three things:

1. Read all of the material on the subject. Often article titles will use a clever trick of relating causation to correlated facts to draw you in. "Does Having More Sex Lead To Higher Wages?" is a prime example. (It doesn't but they are correlated).
2. Use common sense when thinking how A could cause B. How would having more sex make me earn more money? Could it actually just be that people with more money have more sex?
3. Look for supporting evidence. It is rare that you can only find one article on a topic, search and read more. Many things do have causal relationships, but assuming two correlated items have an effect on each other should require some hard data.

Seeing how correlated items are not automatically causally related is a powerful tool to add to your growing toolbox of mental models. When dealing with correlated items always think that they can fall into three different buckets:

1. There is a direct relationship between the two items. (a causal effect)
2. There is an external factor acting on both items (summer ice cream example)
3. There is no relationship and the observance occurred by chance (Nicolas Cage effect)

Tactics vs Strategy

"Strategy without tactics is the slowest route to victory, tactics without strategy is the noise before defeat." —Sun Tsu

The terms tactics and strategy are often used interchangeably in business jargon and online articles, but they are very different. Understanding the difference can be a powerful model for planning.

Strategy - describes the goal and how to reach it
Tactics - are the specific actions to take on the way to the goal

Imagine you are going to climb Mount Everest. Your strategy is to make it to the top, it might also include general items like which side of the mountain you will climb. The tactics are the incremental decisions and actions you will need to take to achieve your strategy, including who you will climb with, where you will camp, what equipment you will bring and learning how to use it properly. Having the strategy is important, but without tactics, you won't be able to achieve it. Having tactics without strategy is equally fruitless since you have no goal to achieve.

To properly leverage these two models it is important to understand how they relate to each other. Here are three ways that strategy and tactics are related to each other and how they are meant to interact:

1. A strategy is long-term and fixed, tactics are short-term and flexible based on the success of the strategy. If your strategy is to win a battle and the original tactics aren't getting it done, changing tactics can improve the odds of reaching the goal of victory.
2. Tactics always have to be in line with the strategy. This can be found out of whack in many large businesses. One department will implement a new project (tactic) and do well with it, despite the fact that it is outside the

scope of the larger business strategy.
3. Tactics and strategy are a means to an end. If the goal changes you have a new strategy and new tactics will follow. Thinking back to the mountain climbing example, if halfway up the accent a climber suffers an injury the strategy changes from reaching the summit to getting safely off the mountain.

This matters when reasoning because it gives you a flexible model to achieve your goals. When facing adversity it becomes possible to change tactics instead of giving up on an overarching strategy.

CHAPTER SIX: NEGOTIATING

Negotiating with others is something many of us avoid. Having a series of mental models to lean on can make a negotiation easier and less combative. The following models are based around finding common ground, and avoiding winner take all type negotiations. Before beginning any discussion that could become contentious it is important to have a defined position and understand what your best case outcome and acceptable outcomes are. After that try internalizing and using the following models.

Third Story

> *When you voice your disagreement, begin by talking about what you have in common with the person you are arguing with. Too often we rush to judgment, race to argue, and overlook all the common ground we share.* - Matthew Kelly

When approaching a negotiation we are often told to put ourselves in the other party's shoes and try to see things from their perspective. The third story is an extension of this, it involves putting yourself in the shoes of a neutral, third-party, such as a mediator and telling a story that all parties can agree upon. By finding a version of the truth where everyone can agree it becomes easier to start negotiating items that are in accord and then move on to other points where there is more distance between the parties.

In their book, "Difficult Conversations: How to Discuss What Matters Most", authors Douglas Stone, Bruce Patton, and Sheila Heen lay out the third story model. "The key is learning to describe the gap—or difference—between your story and the other person's story. Whatever else you may think and feel, you can at least agree that you and the other person see things differently."

It is also important to understand the difference between positions and interests. A position is a fixed idea that each of us has internalized and carries with us. Positions are usually static and unchanging, they include things like political affiliation, religion, and worldview. Interests are somewhat flexible over time. A few examples of interests are personal financial concerns, political issues, and current beliefs. When a negotiation is centered on positions it is difficult to make any progress, instead focusing on interests allows both parties to work towards a compromise that benefits their interests.

Another closely related model is the Most Respectful Interpretation (MRI). Instead of thinking of every action someone else takes in a negative light try to cast it in a positive way, or ignore it. This goes back to Hanlon's Razor and not interpreting anything as malicious automatically.

In the 1960's the US and USSR were in the midst of the Cuban Missile Crisis when JFK used a version of the MRI. The Soviets had made an overture toward de-escalation and then, before a response had been issued, sent another message more hostile in nature. Kennedy choose to ignore the more warlike message and only responded to the original. It turned out that the Soviet Premier had been forced to send it by his more hawkish generals. By assuming the best Kennedy was able to keep communications open, and eventually bring the world back from the brink of war.

Always start a negotiation by understanding where common ground lies. If you are in salary negotiations a good starting point might be to outline how both you and your employer want what is best for the company and its customers. In a political negotiation stating that both parties want peace and prosperity can start discussions from a mutually beneficial perspective.

Approach any potentially contentious negotiation with empathy and understanding of the other side's position, but also an understanding of where both of your interests overlap. By agreeing on some issues it makes finding common ground on others possible.

Zero Sum Game Theory

In a zero-sum game, the problem is entirely one of distribution, not at all one of production. - Kenneth Waltz

Game theory was pioneered in the 1950s by mathematicians Merrill M. Flood and Melvin Dresher, and their earliest work was focused on optimizing success in zero-sum games. Zero-sum means that when one player wins, his opponent loses an equal amount. Think of poker, where when one player wins they get all the chips in the pot, and the other player has lost all the chips they committed to the pot. Most board games are also zero-sum (you can't have both players win a game of chess).

A non-zero sum game offers the ability for all parties to benefit. This is more descriptive of the real world. Two illustrate, imagine a cake. In a zero-sum world if I take a larger slice of cake it means there is less available for everyone else. In a non-zero sum world, we can always go buy another cake, and the amount that everyone gets expands.

In negotiation, thinking of every situation as a zero-sum game can lead us into what social psychologists refer to as "social traps". These are situations where maximizing short-term benefits can lead to long-term losses. Overfishing is a great example of a social trap turning a short-term positive into a big loss for everyone involved.

In the 1960's Canada realized there was a big problem with the cod population in the Grand Banks fishing region. For hundreds of years, people had been fishing in the area commercially and catching a seemingly limitless supply of codfish. By the 1960s things were changing. The government tried to pass laws and prohibitions to limit the annual catch, which were unsuccessful due to pressure from industry lobbying. By 1990 the fish population had crashed and the government was finally able to pass an indefinite moratorium for cod fishing on the Grand Banks in

1992. However, it was too late. Today the entire industry has disappeared due to its short-term win of staying unregulated for 30 years.

Knowing the difference between zero-sum and having the potential for win-win negotiations can be difficult. Always look for the potential to "grow the cake", and take into account long-term outcomes that will result from any decision made.

Framing, Anchoring, and Ordering

"Better a diamond with a flaw than a pebble without." — Confucius

This section deals with assigning value. Value, in its most basic form, is the comparison between two things. If you want to buy a cup of coffee you need to compare your desire for the coffee to your desire to have the asking price worth of money. If I told you a cup of coffee costs $20 you would probably laugh at me, you have internally compared the two and decided you would rather keep your money.

The following models deal with how we can affect and even change that internal comparison. They can even allow us to change the way others assign value. They also let us know when we might be on the other side of the equation and end up over or undervalued.

Framing is the way in which something is defined. To illustrate imagine you are shopping for hamburger meat at the grocery store. Which package would you rather buy?
- One pound of meat that is 10% Fat
- One pound of meat that is 90% Lean

Most people would choose the second, and that is why hamburger meat is labeled as such. The products are identical, but the way they are described elicits different feelings in people. There is a popular toothpaste commercial slogan "recommend by 4 out of 5 dentists". It would have a much different message if the slogan was changed to "20% of dentists don't like this stuff".

Anchoring deals with setting a reference point for comparison, usually by placing lower cost items after a higher cost item. Imagine you are shopping for a new smartphone. You go into a store and look at several models and then choose one that meets your needs, which costs $300. At this point, the salesperson suggests several accessories like a case, a screen protector, etc. Each of these items might cost between $20-$30, but compared to the anchor price they seem cheap. If you were to just buy the phone and then several days later decide to buy a case, you might scoff at $30, but at the moment, during the sale, it doesn't seem expensive.

Anchoring can be seen everywhere. Restaurants will often add an extremely expensive dish or wine to their menu. The goal isn't to sell the most expensive item, but to anchor the consumer's perspective of what the prices should be. Car dealers also engage in anchoring. After agreeing on the price of a car they will begin to try to upsell other items and packages like roadside assistance, satellite radio or the mysterious "undercoating".

Ordering is closely related to anchoring. It describes how the order that different choices are listed informs a customer's perception of value. Going back to the earlier example of a restaurant wine list, if the most expensive bottle of wine is placed first it sets consumers' expectations as they continue to read. According to an article in Atlas Obscura, titled "Does Everyone Really Order the Second-Cheapest Wine?" the reverse is often true. Consumers who aren't wine experts will often order the second least-expensive bottle of wine off the menu to avoid looking cheap. Restaurants know this and respond by making the second cheapest bottle of wine on the menu the one with the highest markup, or a brand they are having trouble selling.

These strategies are very useful in negotiation. By leading with a higher amount than you are prepared to settle for you are setting an anchor. By starting negotiations on issues that are easier to resolve you are ordering in a way that builds trust. And by focusing on points that both parties agree upon you are framing the conversation is a positive, non-zero sum way.

Nash Equilibrium

"A proven theorem of game theory states that every game with complete information possesses a saddle point and therefore a solution." - Richard Arnold Epstein

John Forbes Nash was a mathematician in the 20th century. His work was popularized by Russell Crowe in the movie "A Beautiful Mind". He won the Nobel Prize for Mathematics in 1992. Nash worked in numerous fields but had perhaps the most influence in game theory.

The mental model in this section, the Nash Equilibrium, is a concept to describe a non-cooperative game with two or more players. Assuming that all the players know the rational move that every other player will make, and they will also make a rational move, the game will reach a state of equilibrium. Many theories can be extrapolated from this, including that making a seemingly irrational move may be the best solution, or that it may be better not to play at all.

A simple explanation is given in "A Beautiful Mind". Nash and his friends are in a bar looking at a group of girls. They are all discussing that they are interested in a particularly attractive blonde and how to successfully woo her. According to Nash, the best possible solution is for everyone to ignore her, "If we all go for the blonde," he says, "we block each other and not a single one of us is going to get her. So then we go for her friends, but they will all give us the cold shoulder because nobody likes to be the second choice. But what if no one goes to the blonde? We don't get in each other's way and we don't insult the other girls. That's the only way we win."

A thought experiment called the prisoner's dilemma can also help to show the way the Nash Equilibrium can be gamed out. Imagine two criminals are picked up for a robbery. The police suspect they were both involved, and they are taken to the police station and held in separate rooms. The police interview each man and make the following case. Confess and implicate the other man and you will be let go (providing he does not do the same). If both confess they will each get 5 years in prison. Don't confess and get 10 years if the other man takes the deal. If neither confesses they will each get 1 year in jail for a lesser charge.

Without the option to talk to the other player this becomes a non-cooperative game. It is likely that both confess since it gives the option of either going free or serving only 5 years, and eliminates the chance of serving ten years. Logically it would seem that neither man should confess, but the Nash Equilibrium shows otherwise.

This model can be seen in many places.

Most people agree professional sports would be better off without performance-enhancing drugs. Most athletes who have been caught using these banned substances will tell you they only did them to keep up with everyone else in the league who were already using drugs.

Everyone knows that pollution is bad for the environment. Most companies will agree with this fact, even those in high-pollution industries. Each company derives a financial gain from polluting, and can justify it by saying "if we didn't pollute another company in our industry would".

Understanding the rationale behind the decisions others make is key to leveraging this model. By knowing all the players and their moves before they make them, you have a big advantage in any negotiation. Knowing when to make a counter-intuitive move, or even change the game entirely can be a big advantage and allow you to succeed and break free from a stalemate.

CHAPTER SEVEN: LEARNING

One of the habits most successful people have is they continue learning throughout their entire life. Research shows the actively learning new things keeps the brain more flexible and can even help prevent dementia in the elderly. Learning new skills doesn't have to be a formal process. After many people graduate from school they stop actively learning because of a distaste for classroom environments. Using the models in this chapter you can improve your ability to learn, and the quality of recall.

Dunning-Kruger Effect

"Those who know do not speak. Those who speak do not know." – Lao Tzu

This model is based on the work of psychologists Justin Kruger and David Dunning's 1999 study "Unskilled and Unaware of It: How Difficulties in Recognizing One's Own Incompetence Lead to Inflated Self-Assessments". This study could be called "Too Stupid to Know You Are Stupid" and it deals with the blind spot we all have in accessing our level of intelligence or skill in a new area.

The research that went into this model was conducted on groups of students entering introductory courses into fields they had not studied before. The students were given tests to see how much they already knew about the material and then asked about how well they thought they had done on the tests. Two interesting results emerged, regardless of the field of study in question. The students that did the best on the tests thought they did about average, and the students that did worst on the tests thought they were above average.

Those who have low ability do not have the understanding to see they are lacking ability. Conversely, those who performed the best underestimate their ability, assuming that everyone is able to perform at a similar level.

The Dunning-Kruger effect can also be used to explain the many of the negative effects of overconfidence. The old saying, "a little knowledge is a dangerous thing" applies here. In one of the studies, participants were asked how familiar they were with technical terms, those that said they recognized them were then asked if they were familiar with similar sounding, made-up terms. The majority said they were familiar with the fake terms, even though they didn't actually mean anything.

This effect doesn't mean much in a low-stakes situation, as described in these studies, but there are many instances where limited knowledge has negative real-world outcomes. A person new to financial investing can perceive some initial gains to mean he has figured out the market, and result in big losses. A person who has successfully used a home remedy to treat an ailment might not seek out medical treatment for a serious condition.

Understanding how we actually become proficient in a new field and can avoid early overconfidence is described by Carmen Sanchez of Cornell University and David Dunning of the University of Michigan, in what they called the *"beginner's bubble hypothesis."* They describe the process of gaining proficiency in a new field as having three stages. At first, the subject is uncertain and cautious of the new task. After some initial success the "beginner's bubble" sets in and they become overconfident, which can lead to errors and setbacks. Finally, the subject goes into a "correction" stage where they begin to gain competency and improve on the skill.

The take away from the Dunning-Kruger Effect is that having limited knowledge or skills in an area can be negative. Always assume you know less than others in areas where you are relatively inexperienced. When you pass the point of overconfidence and reach failure is when you actually make the most progress.

Spacing Effect

"Studying is like rowing a boat upstream, not moving forward is to fall behind" — Chinese Proverb

Most people can relate to a common situation that occurs in school: cramming for a test. You had two weeks to prepare, but you put it off until the night before. Now you have 5 hours to learn everything there is to know about statistics, or the Reformation, or photosynthesis...

The problem is that cramming doesn't work. We aren't wired to learn that way. Some people are able to get away with it (I'm not one of these lucky few), but they would be able to retain more and be able to do more with it by spacing out their study sessions. That brings us to the mental model at hand, the Spacing Effect. Essentially the concept is that spacing out repetitions over time produces better recall than doing the same number of repetitions over a shorter duration.

There are many studies and theories as to why this is the case. The majority of the research boils down to two factors. Spacing out learning session prompts the brain to retrieve information. If you have already read a passage the previous day your brain is actively working to fill in the blanks and recall information that you haven't reached in today's study session. If you just read a passage twice in a row your brain doesn't have time to build up this recall functionality.

Spacing also brings contextual variability into play. If you are studying a foreign language you begin by learning a word and its English counterpart as the first step. Later as you learn new words they may be related to the first word and be used in a different context. This allows the brain to create new pathways to recall a word in relation to something it has already built a strong memory of.

Kevin Wagonfoot

To take full advantage of the spacing effect it is important to understand how it works. By reviewing a piece of information as close as possible to forgetting it you create a stronger pathway to remember it. But if you wait too long and the information is forgotten completely and you will need to start over. This case plays out with people who learn a new language and then stop using it, after enough time has passed they are no longer able to understand it.

Deliberate Practice

"So here we have purposeful practice in a nutshell: Get outside your comfort zone but do it in a focused way, with clear goals, a plan for reaching those goals, and a way to monitor your progress. Oh, and figure out a way to maintain your motivation." — Anders Ericsson

I was hesitant to include this model in the book since it has been covered so thoroughly in other books, most notably in Malcolm Gladwell's 10,000 hours rule, in his book, "Outliers". The concept originated from work done by psychologist Anders Ericsson.

Ericsson specializes in the study of peak performance, and how people who are masters in various fields are able to achieve almost superhuman results. His findings make up the basis for deliberate practice.

Before getting into what makes up a deliberate practice routine it is important to understand the difference between someone's potential to accel and their native ability. I am 5'10" and I love to play basketball. Even if I followed all of the best advice relating to deliberate practice and had the best coaches from an early age I still would not be as good at basketball as Larry Bird or Michael Jordan. That isn't to say I couldn't get really really good by following the advice provided by Ericsson, but hard work and training can only do so much. When considering genetics vs. deliberate practice it is helpful to think of them like a game of poker. The hand you are dealt (genetics) plays a role in the outcome, but if you are not skillful enough to play it correctly (practice) you might not have a great outcome. Even a player with an inferior hand can win if they are skillful enough.

Deliberate practice can be broken down into 6 steps, all of which must be taken to assure maximum results.

1. **Motivation** - if you aren't working on a skill that you

really care about chances are you won't follow through and work through the pain and setbacks that are going to occur. Deliberate practice is a model that can only be used on something that you really care about or it will not produce results.

2. Realistic and specific **Goals** - in order to improve you need to have goals and they need to be very specific. In his book, "Peak", Ericsson used the following example of an amateur golfer trying to improve his game: "What exactly do you need to do to slice five strokes off your handicap? One goal might be to increase the number of drives landing in the fairway. That's a reasonably specific goal, but you need to break it down even more: What exactly will you do to increase the number of successful drives? You will need to figure out why so many of your drives are not landing in the fairway and address that by, for instance, working to reduce your tendency to hook the ball. How do you do that? An instructor can give you advice on how to change your swing motion in specific ways. And so on. The key thing is to take that general goal—get better—and turn it into something specific that you can work on with a realistic expectation of improvement." Instead of just having a goal of getting better you need to identify where you can improve and how you will work to improve in that narrow and specific area.

3. **Get out of your comfort zone** - this step is the most difficult for many people. If you are not constantly challenging yourself and pushing limits then you are not engaged in deliberate practice. In a study of competitive figure skaters, Eriksson found that those who spent more time working on jumps they had not yet mastered did much better in competition than skaters who practiced routines they had already mastered more frequently. Think back to when you were learning to tie your shoes, at first it took concentration and

was difficult to do. Today you can easily tie your shoes without thinking. You don't consider yourself "practicing knots" every time you tie your shoes. If you don't practice out of your comfort zone then you are just repeating a skill you have already become proficient at.
4. **Consistent and persistent** - Deliberate practice requires a schedule and sticking to it. Because the process can be uncomfortable it must be based on a schedule, or it would be too easy to skip days and lose momentum. As we learned in the previous section on the spacing effect, that repeating learning over time re-enforces it and helps recall. Depending on the skill being learned the amount of time spent in practice and the spacing between practice sessions will vary.
5. **Get feedback** - The step could also be called coaching. Without getting feedback it is impossible to know if improvements are being made. Feedback allows you to pinpoint problem areas and then built measurable and specific goals to improve them.
6. Allow time for **Recovery** - because deliberate practice is so intense it is important to schedule downtime for recovery.

The most important factor in deliberate practice is having the desire and passion for the activity. This will carry you through the tedium and setbacks the rest of the process entails. Achieving world-class results is far more than just putting in the hours. While you might not be able to reach the level of a professional athlete, deliberate practice is the most effective way to reach your own maximum ability.

Gamification

"Games are the only force in the known universe that can get people to take actions against their self-interest, in a predictable way, without using force." – Gabe Zimmermann

Gamification is the process of adding game mechanics to an already existing activity or product to increase the level of use or compliance. That is a pretty confusing definition, right? Basically, gamification is adding a level of competition to something that is already being done in order to improve the outcome. Think of a sale contest at a business. The sales people are already making sales, adding a prize that goes to the top earner just makes the job more competitive and fun (at least for the winner).

The reason gamification works is that it leverages several innate human motivations that exist in all of us. These can include:
- Community - success can lead to recognition by the group
- Achievement/Reward - Winning or completing the gamified activity can have some type of prize
- Feedback - even if the game has no "winner" it is favorable to get feedback. This is the reason we watch Jeopardy at home, even though viewers can't win prizes for right answers.

Essentially when something is gamified achievements that are reached release dopamine in the brain. This is the same reason we all check our cell phones constantly throughout the day. Each new piece of information we discover delivers a small hit of dopamine.

The good news is that by controlling how we use gamification we can use this trick to help make better choices. One of the simplest, low-tech ways to gamify anything is through the use of a checklist. Every time you cross off an item as completed, a small hit of dopamine is released to your brain. Don't believe me? Try a simple experiment next time you do your laundry. Make a checklist that day and put the word "Laundry" on it. Keep in mind the task of doing laundry entails multiple steps (washing, drying, folding, ironing, putting away in drawers and on hangers, etc). When you are completely finished and every last garment has been put away you can now cross off the word "Laundry" from your list. Now think how that feeling compares to other times you have done laundry without the checklist involved.

Many businesses use this tactic to get us to stay involved with their company at a higher frequency. My local coffee shop offers a "buy 10 and the 11th coffee is free" promotion, that keeps me from trying the new place down the street. Buying that 10th coffee, releases a big hit of dopamine since it is something that takes a long time to complete. It also makes the 11th coffee seem like a big reward, even though in reality I only saved $2.50.

Other than keeping your clothes clean and fresh smelling you can also gamify many other every day beneficial activities. Think of things in your life you have been trying to improve, some examples could be diet, personal finances, or exercise. Try adding gamification elements and see if they improve your level of adherence.

CHAPTER EIGHT: BUSINESS

This chapter includes four mental models that are primarily used in business and economics but can be applied in many broader contexts.

Opportunity Cost

"In economics, one of the most important concepts is 'opportunity cost' - the idea that once you spend your money on something, you can't spend it again on something else." - Malcolm Turnbull

Opportunity cost is the tradeoff you make when you make a choice. After high school, I decided to go to college instead of entering the workforce directly. The opportunity cost was the tuition I was paying and wages I was losing in order to get a college degree (and earn more later in life). Every choice and every decision has an opportunity cost. If you decide to do "A" you can't also do "B" at the same time.

People generally fail to see opportunity costs present in almost every part of their lives. If you spend money on something, you can't also spend it on something else. If you watch TV every day after work you can't also use that time to practice a hobby or learn a new skill. Even eating habits have opportunity costs, you have a finite appetite for each meal if you eat junk you have less available space for healthy foods.

Training yourself to consider opportunity costs is actually easier to implement than most of the other mental models we have discussed in this book. I can best describe the mental calculation as a simple mathematical formula, although there generally are not numbers available for the calculation. The formula is:

What you need to give up / What you stand to gain = Opportunity cost

As an example we can go back to the college example I mentioned before. After high school, I decided to continue my education instead of getting a job. I stood to gain a college education, and potentially a higher salary in the future. I had to give up time and earnings potential when I was in school. You could try to assign numbers to each item, find out how much more someone with my degree earns per year than someone with a high school diploma, but just by picturing the formula it gives you a new way to visualize the choice.

This is arguably the most important model for evaluating how to allocate resources in a business. If you decide to invest time or money in one part of the business, those resources cannot be allocated in another. Charlie Munger has a great quote about opportunity costs, and how Berkshire Hathaway evaluates opportunities, *"We know we've got opportunity X, which is better than the new opportunity. Why do we want to waste two seconds thinking about the new opportunity?"*

The next time you make a decision take into account what you are giving up when you decide to go with your choice. The opportunity cost might not only be an amount of money or time, it could also be a health outcome, a friendship, a new skill or hobby, or any number of other things. Making a decision to do something, also means you are making a decision not to do something else. Leveraging this mental model means you are considering not just the choice of saying yes to one option, but also saying no to every other competing option as well.

Pygmalion Effect

"A leader's job is not to put greatness into people, but rather to recognize that it already exists, and to create an environment where that greatness can emerge and grow." — Brad Smith

The Pygmalion effect is also known by another name, the self-fulfilling prophecy. In business, it can be described as higher expectations leading to better performance. It was named after a Greek myth about Pygmalion who created a sculpture that was so beautiful and lifelike that he fell in love with it.

There have been several studies that have documented this effect. The most well known was the Rosenthal–Jacobson study, which was conducted on grade school children and their teachers. Researchers did IQ tests on all students at the beginning of the school year, and then selected 20% of each class at random. The selected students were then described to their teachers as high IQ individuals who were going to do well that school year. At the end of the school year all of the students were given another IQ test. It turned out that the 20% of students identified to the teachers made the most significant gains that year, despite having no other advantages over their classmates. The only reason they performed better was that teachers thought they would and treated them accordingly.

One of the most striking examples of this effect can be told through the story of a horse in the late 1800s. William Von Osten was a horse trainer who came across a particularly smart horse name Clever Hans. The horse was able to count, answer simple questions and even do basic math problems. To communicate Clever Hans would stomp his hoof to give the correct answer. The spectacle of a horse who could understand human language and answer questions began to draw in interested spectators, and eventually, the scientific community took an interest. Researchers began studying the horse, looking for signs of trickery but were unable to find any. The horse was even able to answer questions when Von Osten was not present. It appeared that there was no explanation to Clever Hans other than that of a very intelligent horse!

After several years a team of psychologists began to uncover the truth behind Clever Hans. The horse was unable to answer questions correctly if the person asking the question did not know the answer, or if Hans was unable to see the questioner. It turned out that Clever Hans did not understand what was being asked of him at all. He was simply reading the questioner and responding to tiny, non-verbal cues. For example, when the horse was asked for the solution of two plus five he would begin stomping his foot. As he got closer to seven the person asking the question would get more excited and their body language would give away the correct solution.

While Clever Hans presents an interesting story, the effect whose study he spawned can benefit us all. The Pygmalion effect can be seen in many performance-based interactions. When employees are treated with respect and their superiors have high expectations good results generally follow. The opposite effect is also true. Lower expectations often lead to poor performance.

To take advantage of this model understand how your actions and expectations feed into the production and abilities of others. You can also benefit by realizing how others around you (especially superiors) can affect your performance. The simple knowledge that we don't operate in a vacuum and that actions and attitudes have wide-ranging outcomes is the key take away from this model.

Peter Principle

"In time, every post tends to be occupied by an employee who is incompetent to carry out its duties." — Laurence J. Peter

This model comes from the 1970 book written by Laurence J. Peter and Raymond Hull, titled "The Peter Principle". The book is written to be a satire, but the underlying concept resonates with workers in large organizations. Its main concept is that individuals within a large organization will continue to be promoted until they reach a job level they are unable to effectively perform.

Imagine a salesman in a large organization. He is great at sales and thus gets promoted to manager. Being a manager requires a different skill set, which he eventually masters and becomes a great manager. Now he is promoted to being a district manager. This new promotion requires another new skill set, which he is unable to perform or learn. Because he is not doing great at the job he will not be promoted again, but since he has been with the business and done a great job in the past he will not be fired or demoted. He has risen to his level of incompetence.

On a long enough timeline and with a big enough organization every position will be occupied by someone who is too incompetent to perform it correctly. To describe it another way, if your company is managed from the top down, and promotions are based on merit, then everyone in the company will eventually end up one promotion above their level of competence.

To avoid the Peter Principle in business there are three things to be aware of;

1. Most entry-level jobs are specialized or technical in nature. These skills do not necessarily directly translate to management positions.
2. People are drawn to employment in organizations that promote internally. Entry level jobs with no upside po-

tential tend to have a low fulfillment rate.
3. Performance in a current role is generally the consideration for a promotion, as opposed to suitability for the new role.

While the Peter Principle is generally applied to business and hierarchical organizations it can also be seen in our day to day lives. I see it in some of my own issues with lack of focus and project creep. Sometimes when I start a new project I have a lot of enthusiasm and grand ambitions. Concepts and features are continually added to the project scope and the idea of what I want to carry out becomes massive. Since there is no focus on the scope of the project it becomes too large to tackle, and it is never completed. If I had limited my ambition to an attainable goal progress could be made, and eventually, other features could be added. Without careful planning and limiting scope projects can grow too massive and collapse in on themselves under their own weight.

Circle of Competence

"Everybody's got a different circle of competence. The important thing is not how big the circle is. The important thing is staying inside the circle." — Warren Buffett

This is one of my favorite models from Charlie Munger, it describes the way he and Warren Buffett choose investment opportunities at Berkshire Hathaway. Instead of understanding everything about every company in the world, they focus on the areas they understand better than other people and only choose investments that fit into their fields of expertise.

An individual's circle of competence can be drawn from all parts of their life, education, work, hobbies, sports, as well as the products or services they use. Having a high level of knowledge in a particular area gives you an unfair advantage to compete based on that knowledge. Imagine you own a trick deck of cards, where every card has a certain marking on the back that only someone very familiar with the deck can identify. If you are competent at reading the cards you have a massive advantage playing poker with them. Similarly, if you know everything there is to know about investing in the steel industry you have a massive advantage over the other investors with less information and understanding.

Problems arise when you attempt to play outside the circle. Just because someone is an expert in one field they can get a false sense of confidence operating in another area they actually have no understanding or competitive advantage in.

The most important part of the circle of competence model is knowing the edge of your circle. Anything outside of your actual area of expertise, something you think you know, is an area where mistakes can happen. Growing your circle by acquiring

Kevin Wagonfoot

new skills and information is important, but not as important as knowing where the edge of your circle lies.

CONCLUSION

I hope you have enjoyed this look at the world of mental models and found at least a few that can benefit you in your life, work, or personal relationships. I've created a Bonus PDF to this book which has a list of all the mental models discussed, a short description of each and a relevant quote. It is a handy way to keep track of each model and to utilize them in the appropriate situations.

If you enjoyed this book I'd like love to get your feedback in a review, and to recommend a few of my other works. They generally focus on the "Inversion" model of reversing a problem to find new and unique solutions:

Anti-Goals

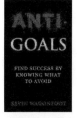

The mental model of inversion is examined in depth.

Anti-Diet

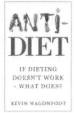

Applying the concept of inversion to healthy eating and a better lifestyle.

Anti-Debt

Building a more sustainable relationship with money by knowing what to avoid.

Anti-Quit

Using counterintuitive techniques to stay motivated and become more "gritty"

Thanks for taking the time,

Kevin Wagonfoot

Made in the USA
Middletown, DE
17 July 2020